MOZART

GREAT LIVES IN GRAPHICS

Button
Books

Johannes Chrysostomus Wolfgangus Theophilus Mozart, better known as Wolfgang Amadeus Mozart, is one of the greatest composers of all time. He started playing piano and violin at just three years old and was writing music by the time he was five. But all that talent doesn't mean he didn't have to work hard, too. The music he wrote when he was young was good, but the pieces he wrote when he was older, after years of practice and tremendous hard work, are out of this world.

And that's what makes them, and him, so special. The more you read about Mozart, the more you realize how much more there is to learn. He loved making rude jokes, he made fun of the upper classes, and his life wasn't always easy. He wasn't good with money, he loved to party and buy frivolous clothes, but he also worked so hard his hands became deformed. He was the ultimate child prodigy with a breathtaking gift. But he was also an ordinary boy whose drive and determination allowed him to create some of the most incredible music ever written.

MOZART'S WORLD

1765 James Watt develops steam engine

1764
Composes first symphony. Taught by Bach's son, Johann Christian

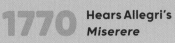

1767
Composes first opera

1756
Born on January 27 in Salzburg, Austria. Seven Years' War begins

1769
Goes on tour in Italy

1759 Starts to play harpsichord age 3

1762
Catherine the Great is Empress of All Russia. Mozart tours Europe

1770 Hears Allegri's *Miserere*

1773 Boston Tea Party

1776
Declaration of Independence on July 4

1760
George III is British King; Industrial Revolution begins

1777
Leaves Salzburg, starts journey to Paris

1786
Composes *Marriage of Figaro*

1787
Composes *Don Giovanni*. Possibly meets Beethoven. Father dies

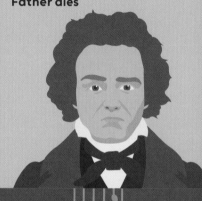

1778
Mozart's mother dies. Captain Cook arrives in Hawaii

1786
First ascent of Mont Blanc

1785
Dollar becomes currency of US

1781
Uranus discovered

1784
Son Karl Thomas is born

1789
French Revolution. George Washington is President of US

1782
Marries Constanze Weber

1791
Son Franz Xaver born. Composes *The Magic Flute*

1783
First hot air balloon flight

DIES
December 5 in Vienna, Austria

The family lived squeezed together in a one-bedroom apartment on the third floor of a house in Salzburg. Today the house is one of the most visited museums in Austria.

Happy FAMILIES

Mozart was very close to his family. One of seven children born to Anna Maria and Leopold Mozart, he and his older sister Maria Anna (known as Nannerl) were the only two to survive. Their dad was a violin teacher and everything they did was accompanied by music, from walking between rooms to playing with toys.

PET SANCTUARY

They had several pets, including a cat, a canary, a grasshopper, and the family dog, Pimperl.

Leopold
FATHER

Leopold was a loving but strict father. He worked as a composer for the Prince-Archbishop, who lived in a palace overlooking the town.

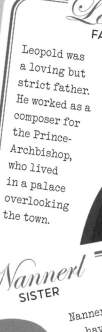

Nannerl
SISTER

Nannerl may have been equally talented as Mozart, but girls at that time weren't encouraged to write music or allowed to perform after the age of 18.

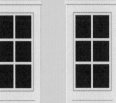

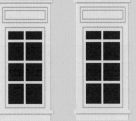

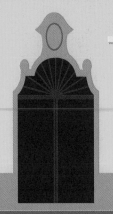

Mozart didn't go to school. When Leopold realized how good a musician Mozart could be, he gave up his job to teach him full-time. As well as music, his dad taught him several languages—English, French, Italian, Latin, and his native German—plus geography, science, history, and math.

Every Sunday the family played a game called Bölzlschiessen, where they shot darts at circular wooden targets with an air gun. The targets could be as big as 3 ft (1m)-wide, with a painted picture and a poem that poked fun at someone they knew!

$$a^2 + b^2 = c^2$$

Carpe diem
et cetera

$1 \times 3 = 3$
$2 \times 3 = 6$
$3 \times 3 = 9$
✓ *well done Wolfgang*

I ♡ math

After music, Mozart loved math the most. According to a family friend, "when he was doing sums, the table, the chair, the walls, and even the floor would be covered with chalked numbers."

DID YOU KNOW?

Mozart's home would have had no running water or electricity and chamber pots in the bedroom.

At the time it was thought lower-class to breastfeed a baby, so Mozart was fed barley water instead. He and his sister grew up small, pale, and sickly.

Mozart's dad quickly realized his two young children were musical prodigies and that money was to be made. When Mozart was six and Nannerl 10, he took them on a tour of Europe to perform for royalty. Nannerl was talented but Mozart turned out to be the one to watch. "All the ladies are in love with my boy," boasted Leopold, who acted as his agent, booking shows and selling souvenirs as they wowed audiences everywhere they went.

TRAVELING CIRCUS

Gallivanting all over Europe showing off to kings and queens might sound like fun, but back in the 18th century travel wasn't easy. There were no planes, trains, or cars. Mozart would have been stuck in a horse-drawn carriage with his family for hours on end bouncing over bumpy dirt roads. Carriages were freezing in winter and too hot in summer, and many would get stuck in mud in the middle of nowhere. Thieves and highwaymen often lurked waiting to pounce in ambush.

While playing at concerts in Paris, Mozart published his first piece of music: a violin sonata. He was eight. Shops would sell the music to people who wanted to play it at home.

SPEED OF CARRIAGE **5** *MPH (8KM/H)*

The route from Salzburg to Munich would have taken

 **DAYS** *in* **MOZART'S TIME**

ONLY 90 MINUTES ON THE MOTORWAY TODAY

Child prodigies were rare in Mozart's time, so when he performed in

LONDON AGED 8

people couldn't believe a child could be so good at the piano and accused him of being a dwarf.

Mozart caught smallpox while traveling and, according to his sister Nannerl, was so ill he couldn't see for nine days! He spent his recovery time learning card tricks and fencing.

Smallpox was a terrible disease that gave you huge blisters and killed many people. Thankfully today it's been wiped out by vaccines.

At one concert in Munich, Mozart and his sister played together for

3 HOURS STRAIGHT

Mozart lived for 35 years, 10 months, and nine days (13,088 days). For 10 years, two months, and eight days (3,720 days) of that time he was on tour!

London
Amsterdam
Haarlem
The Hague
Utrecht
Dover
Antwerp
Ghent
Calais
Brussels
Cologne
Lille
Liège
Mainz
Frankfurt
Mannheim
Paris
Munich
Dijon
Salzburg
Zürich
Geneva
Lyon

Dear Dad

Mozart's dad, Leopold, was a great letter writer who loved to hoard information, make lists, and keep diaries. Some of this must have rubbed off on the young Mozart, because the two of them wrote hundreds of letters to each other. Filled with funny jokes and secret codes, those that survive today reveal how musical Mozart was, but also how quirky and mischievous.

The Mozarts shared a love of toilet humor. His mom was always making rude comments and Mozart's letters are full of rhyming poop jokes!

Mozart adored his mom. He wrote to her:

"I kiss your hand 100,000 times. I can't fit any more zeroes on the page."

Mozart often jokingly signed his letters

TRAZOM GNAGFLOW

It's his name backward.

DID YOU KNOW?

An anagram of
WOLFGANG AMADEUS MOZART
is
A FAMOUS GERMAN WALTZ GOD

He wrote to his sister:

"Write to me and don't be so lazy. Otherwise I shall have to give you a thrashing. What fun! I'll break your head."

DIE ZEITUNG

MOZART LOVED WORDS

almost as much as music and liked to make up funny poems and anagrams.

Exclusive!

He wrote a series of riddles and proverbs that became so popular they were even published in a newspaper.

CONFIDENTIAL

Secret Codes

TOP SECRET

In the 18th century lots of letters were opened and read by the government, and people who had new ideas about religion or politics could be arrested by the secret police. Knowing this, the Mozarts created their own secret code to keep some of the things they wrote private.

Mozart and his dad wrote
114+ LETTERS HOME
while they were traveling in Italy. In them they mentioned:

452 people

42 of Mozart's works

173 places

50 works by other composers

303 locations

PIANO MAN

Mozart's favorite instrument was the piano. He was a perfectionist who practiced for hours every day. Look at how many things the brain has to do at once while you play piano...

EYES

You need to read two lines of music, each with different notes.

Mozart's first piano had no pedals and the color of the keys was reversed.

SPACE

You learn where the keys are without having to look.

HANDS

Each hand plays independently from the other.

L R

FEET

The left and right foot operate different pedals.

Around

750,000

pianos are made throughout the world every year.

EARS

As you hear the notes you're playing you make changes to what you're doing.

EMOTIONS

Playing louder, softer, faster, or slower makes people feel certain emotions.

FINGERS

The piano is one of the few instruments where you use all 10 fingers.

TIMING

Your brain monitors everything and keeps the beat.

DID YOU KNOW?

88 KEYS

Usually there aren't more than **88 KEYS** on a piano. Bartolomeo Cristofori's pianoforte had 54 keys. As piano music developed, more keys were added and by the 1890s keyboards had 88, the same as today. Notes played above or below the 88 keys are too high and low for the human ear to hear properly. When more keys are added, the lower notes sound like a rumbling noise and the higher notes can be jarring.

---

c900
DULCIMER

One of the piano's earliest ancestors was first used in the Middle East. Players would use two sticks to hammer strings on a soundboard.

c1400
CLAVICHORD

The clavichord became popular just before Mozart's time. Small and simple with a quiet sound, when a key was pressed a brass blade would hit a pair of strings.

c1440
HARPSICHORD

Mozart played the harpsichord as a child. It looked a bit like a piano but plucked the strings instead of hitting them when a key was pressed.

c1700
PIANOFORTE

Invented by Bartolomeo Cristoferi, this early version of today's piano hit the strings like a clavichord but became more popular because it could make a soft and a loud sound.

HOW WE HEAR

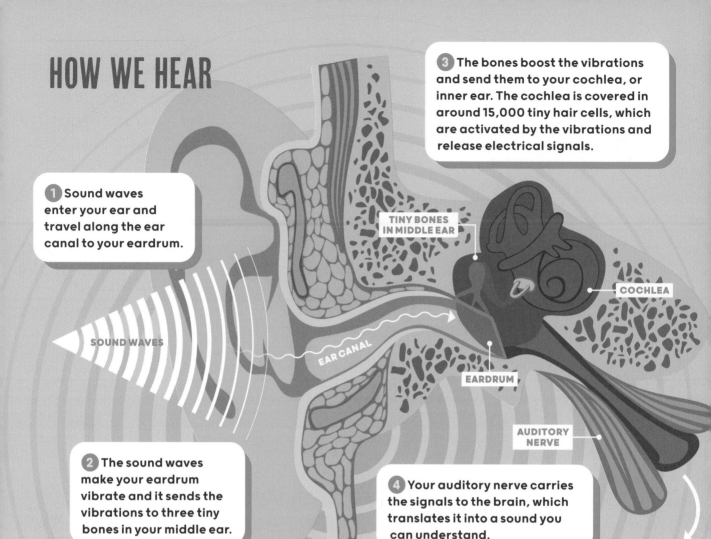

3 The bones boost the vibrations and send them to your cochlea, or inner ear. The cochlea is covered in around 15,000 tiny hair cells, which are activated by the vibrations and release electrical signals.

1 Sound waves enter your ear and travel along the ear canal to your eardrum.

TINY BONES IN MIDDLE EAR

COCHLEA

SOUND WAVES

EAR CANAL

EARDRUM

AUDITORY NERVE

2 The sound waves make your eardrum vibrate and it sends the vibrations to three tiny bones in your middle ear.

4 Your auditory nerve carries the signals to the brain, which translates it into a sound you can understand.

TO BRAIN

GOOD VIBRATIONS

When Mozart was around four years old, his dad noticed he had "perfect pitch." That's what people call it when you can sing any note without being played one first as a starting point. So if you were asked to sing a G, you could just do it on the spot. Some people think you have to be born with perfect pitch, but others believe you can learn it through training. Apparently Mozart's pitch was so perfect, instruments that were out of tune made him cry!

Hundreds of years ago, the Vatican (home to the Pope) asked Italian composer Allegri to write a song that would only be played in its Sistine Chapel. The song he wrote was called *Miserere*, and it was kept a secret for almost 150 years. That was until 14-year-old Mozart heard the piece. Legend has it he rushed home and wrote down the entire work from memory, producing the first unauthorized copy of the song!

Someone who saw Mozart play just before he toured Europe wrote:

— 66 —

I saw and heard how, when he was made to listen in another room, they would give him notes, now high, now low, not only on the pianoforte but on every other imaginable instrument as well, and he came out with the letter of the name of the note in an instant. Indeed, on hearing a bell toll, or a clock or even a pocket watch strike, he was able at the same moment to name the note of the bell or time piece

— 99 —

PERFECT PITCH

J.S. Bach

Beethoven

It's thought other great classical composers like Bach, Händel, Chopin, and Beethoven had the gift as well.

Pop singer Mariah Carey has it, as did Jimi Hendrix, Ella Fitzgerald, and Bing Crosby.

Mariah Carey

Jimi Hendrix

Ella Fitzgerald

Bing Crosby

Bats, wolves, dogs, gerbils and birds appear to have perfect pitch too!

FEWER THAN
1 IN 10,000 PEOPLE HAVE PERFECT PITCH

People who have this strange ability may start to
LOSE IT AROUND 40 YEARS OLD

Even those born with perfect pitch need to be
AROUND MUSIC AS A CHILD, or it won't develop.

BOY WONDER

AGE 3
Plays chords on clavichord and harpsichord, learns to play violin.

AGE 4
Takes just

1/2 HOUR

to learn a minuet.

Mozart showed an incredible talent for music from a young age. Some people have called him gifted, but don't forget that he also worked tremendously hard. He became an expert at piano, organ, and violin and could play pretty much every other instrument in the orchestra well enough to compose–that

AGE 11
Writes first opera, *Apollo et Hyacinthus*, and first piano concerto.

1ST

AGE 12
Composes another opera:

La finta semplice

AGE 14
Hears Allegri's *Miserere* while visiting Rome and writes it down from memory.

AGE
5
Writes first piece of music.

1ST

AGE
6
1ST

ADMIT ONE

PERFORMS AT
CONCERT
for
FIRST TIME

ADMIT ONE

AGE
8
Writes first symphony; publishes first piece of music.

1ST

would have taken years of practice! He attended concerts most nights, hung out with famous musicians, and was always listening to other people's work, plus he wrote and rewrote his own works many times to get them right. In the end his hard work paid off—the pieces he wrote changed the way people played music forever.

AGE
15
Says that he is hearing whole operas "at home in my head."

AGE
18

COMPOSES 30TH SYMPHONY

DID YOU KNOW?

True child prodigies are very rare. A recent study estimates that real prodigies are as uncommon as 1 in every 10 million people!

10M

Sometimes Mozart would spend

15 HOURS/DAY WRITING MUSIC

Apparently his hands became so deformed from writing, eventually he couldn't even cut his own food!

GREATEST HITS

Clarinet Concerto

His clarinet concerto was **more advanced** than anything written for the instrument before.

▶❚❚

Mozart had an ear for a great tune. His livelihood depended on people coming to hear his operas and they did so more often if the melody was memorable. The musical style he created–using simple harmonies and three or four major chords–can still be heard in rock and pop songs today.

THE *Magic* FLUTE

MOST FAMOUS

This is one of Mozart's most famous operas. You'd probably recognize the part called the **birdcatcher's song** if you heard it.

Marriage of Figaro

Mozart understood people's characters very well and included some **clever moments** in this opera when several people sing at once, each **showing their view of the situation**.

AT LEAST **626** WORKS **INCLUDING** ➤	**50** SYMPHONIES	**27** PIANO CONCERTOS	**5** VIOLIN CONCERTOS	**35** CONCERT ARIAS	**23** STRING QUARTETS	**18** MASSES	**22** OPERAS
	𝄞				♪♪♪♪	✝	

JUPITER SYMPHONY No.41

When Mozart was young, symphonies were short, relatively simple pieces of music. He turned them into half-an-hour masterpieces.

DON GIOVANNI

Rumor has it the night before the deadline for this opera Mozart still hadn't written its introduction. He tried to stay awake and finish it but fell asleep on the couch until 5am. He awoke suddenly, dashed out the overture, and **delivered it on time just two hours later.**

PLAYING BY EAR

Mozart was amazing at improvisation– making up music as he went along. Because of this, some of his compositions have blank space where the piano music should be. He saved himself the time of writing all the music out and just improvised on stage!

Meaning **A Little Night Music**, this was written for string instruments and can be heard everywhere from **movies** to **cell phone ringtones**.

SERENADE No. 13

"EINE KLEINE NACHTMUSIK"

Mozart mixtape

Turkish Rondo

Taken from a **piano sonata,** this is one of his best-known tunes.

DID YOU KNOW?

If you were to listen to all of Mozart's music back to back, it would take you

202 HOURS that's more than **8 DAYS**

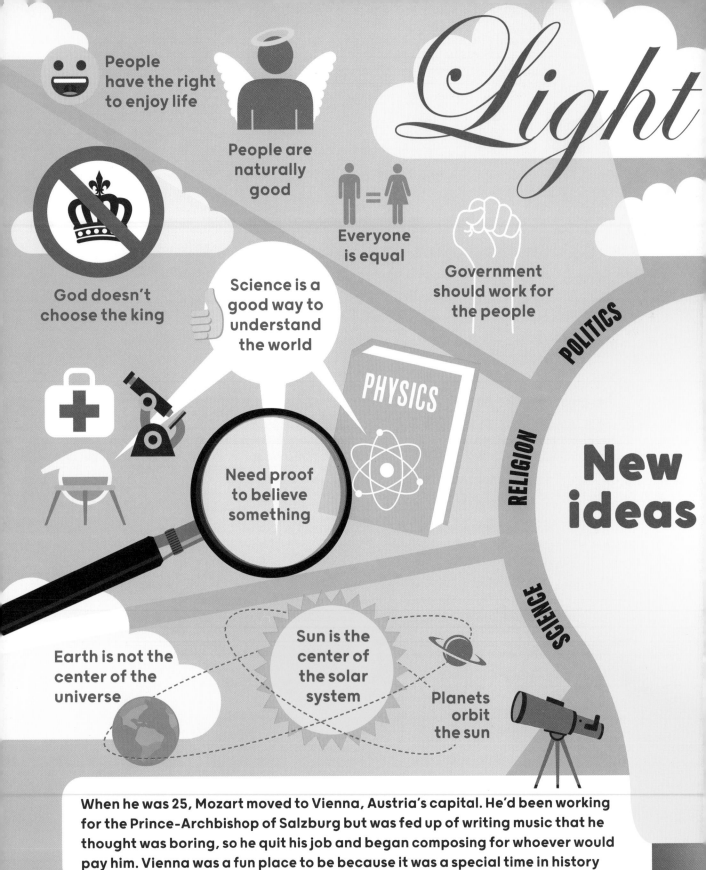

People have the right to enjoy life

People are naturally good

Everyone is equal

Government should work for the people

God doesn't choose the king

Science is a good way to understand the world

Light

Need proof to believe something

PHYSICS

POLITICS

RELIGION

New ideas

SCIENCE

Earth is not the center of the universe

Sun is the center of the solar system

Planets orbit the sun

When he was 25, Mozart moved to Vienna, Austria's capital. He'd been working for the Prince-Archbishop of Salzburg but was fed up of writing music that he thought was boring, so he quit his job and began composing for whoever would pay him. Vienna was a fun place to be because it was a special time in history

Fantastic

POLAND

GERMANY

VIENNA

AUSTRIA

ITALY

People don't make good decisions

People need kings to rule them

POLITICS

The church knows everything

RELIGION

Old ideas

God chooses the king

SCIENCE

Earth is flat

Earth is center of universe

Oceans are full of sea monsters

called the Age of Enlightenment. Poets, musicians, and scientists were coming up with new ideas about politics and religion, and in the evenings there were fabulous masked balls and operas. Mozart played the piano at parties all over town, strutting his stuff in gold-trimmed hats and red coats with pearl buttons.

FAMILY TREE

MOZARTS

MOM
Anna Maria
Pertl

DAD
Leopold
Mozart

BROTHER
Johann Leopold
Joachim

SISTER
Maria Anna
Cordula

SISTER
Maria Anna
Nepomucena
Walpurgis

SISTER
Maria Anna
(Nannerl)

BROTHER
Johann Karl
Amadeus

SISTER
Maria Crescentia
Francisca de
Paula

DID YOU KNOW?

MOZART'S SON KARL had a daughter but she died aged 10, possibly from smallpox.

HIS OTHER SON FRANZ didn't have any children, so

MOZART HAS NO DIRECT DESCENDANTS

GENIUS
Wolfgang
Amadeus

ALMOST 1/2 OF CHILDREN
DIED
BEFORE THEIR
5TH BIRTHDAY
IN THE 18TH CENTURY!

People didn't know germs caused disease.

There were no antibiotics or vaccines.

Busy mothers couldn't always watch infants who fell down wells, into fires, or were hit by carts on the street.

SON
Raimund
Leopold

SON
Karl Thomas

SON
Johann Thomas
Leopold

Not long after Mozart arrived in Vienna, he moved in with the Weber family as a lodger. He fell in love with their daughter Aloysia, but when she rejected him he started courting one of her younger sisters, Constanze. Against his father's wishes he married her and she turned out to be the love of his life.

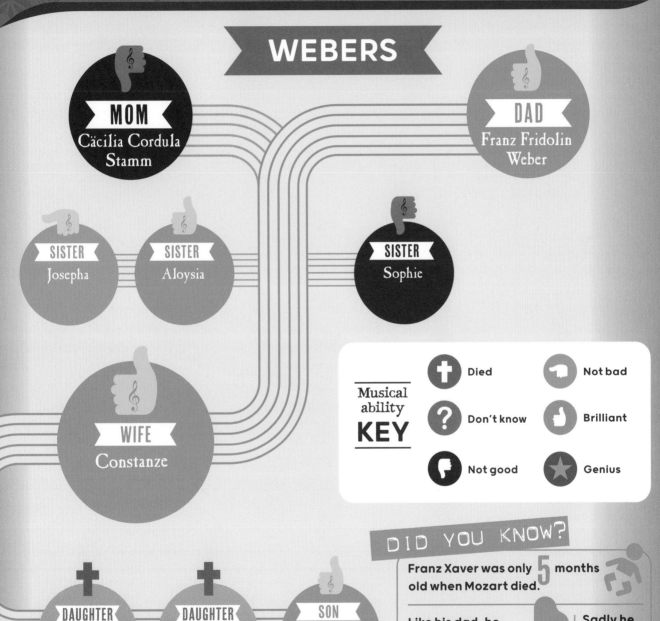

WEBERS

MOM
Cäcilia Cordula Stamm

DAD
Franz Fridolin Weber

SISTER
Josepha

SISTER
Aloysia

SISTER
Sophie

WIFE
Constanze

Musical ability KEY

✝ Died
? Don't know
👎 Not good
🤚 Not bad
👍 Brilliant
⭐ Genius

DAUGHTER
Theresia Constantia Adelhaid Friederica Marianna

DAUGHTER
Anna Maria

SON
Franz Xaver Wolfgang

DID YOU KNOW?

Franz Xaver was only 5 months old when Mozart died.

Like his dad, he learned piano and violin, started composing very young, and made his first public performance aged 13.

Sadly he died from cancer at the age of 53

Love bird

MOZART LOVED BIRDS.

For a while his family had a canary and other birds as pets, and Mozart would ask after them in his letters home. But it was his pet starling that captured his heart.

Constant companion

3 YEARS

Cost

34 KREUZER

...a silver coin that was a unit of currency in Austria at the time.

EQUIVALENT TO

$11
TODAY

When starlings flock together it's called a murmuration. One of Britain's greatest

wildlife spectacles, a murmuration of six million birds was spotted in Somerset, UK in 1999.

MOZART TAUGHT THE STARLING TO SING the opening to his piano concerto Number 17.

MOZART WAS CROSS when the starling added an extra note and sang a G-sharp instead of a G!

MOZART WAS 28 when he bought the starling from a pet store in Vienna.

Funeral march

About a week after his dad died on May 28, 1787, Mozart's starling passed away. Mozart hadn't been able to go home to Salzburg for his father's funeral because it was too far, but he made up for it with an elaborate ceremony for the starling. He gathered his friends in front of the tiny graveside, which was marked with a headstone. Wearing veils they marched around it singing hymns and Mozart recited a special poem he'd written for the occasion:

Here rests a bird called Starling,
A foolish little darling.
He was still in his prime
When he ran out of time,
And my sweet little friend
Came to a bitter end,
Creating a terrible smart
Deep in my heart.
Gentle Reader! Shed a tear,
For he was dear,
Sometimes a bit too jolly
And, at times, quite folly,
But nevermore
A bore.
I bet he is now up on high
Praising my friendship to the sky,
Which I render
Without tender;
For when he took his sudden leave,
Which brought to me such grief,
He was not thinking of
the man
Who writes and rhymes
as no one can.

MOZART, JUNE 4, 1787

✝ DAD MAY 28 1787

R.I.P.
STARLING

JUNE, 1787

HAIR RAISING!
A lock of Mozart's hair once sold at auction for
$48,000

WOLFGANG AMADEUS
MOZART

Born
1756

Features

INTENSE EYES   LARGE HEAD

First instruments
HARPSICHORD, VIOLIN

Court composer
AGE 31

AUSTRIAN

Piano concertos
27

Operas
22

Hated
Trumpets

Loved
Playing billiards, spending money

Almost taught
BEETHOVEN

Height
5 FT 4 IN
(163cm)

FALSE ALARM
Mozart was **TERRIFIED OF TRUMPETS** as a child. His dad tried to cure him by having a friend blow a trumpet at him until he realized they weren't scary, but it didn't work. I wonder why?

Died
POOR

Legacy

MOST FAMOUS COMPOSER IN WORLD

ANTONIO SALIERI

Not everything was rosy in Mozart's world. According to legend, he had an arch-rival who whispered nasty things about him behind his back and sometimes made it difficult for him to get work–Italian composer Antonio Salieri.

ITALIAN

Operas
43

Piano concertos
2

Height
5 FT 7 IN
(170cm)

Died **RICH**

Taught
**BEETHOVEN
SCHUBERT
LISZT**

First instruments
HARPSICHORD, VIOLIN

Court composer
AGE 24

Hated
Drinking alcohol

Loved
Eating candy and cake

DID YOU KNOW?

Some say Salieri was so envious of Mozart's talent that he was the one who **POISONED** him. But experts now think that these were just rumors.

Born
1750

Features
QUICK-TEMPERED   BLACK HAIR

!@X#?

Legacy

LARGELY FORGOTTEN

BRAIN POWER

MEMORY
Helps you to remember things

FEEL
Can speed healing and relieve pain

MOOD
Reduces stress and anxiety

Your **BRAIN ON MUSIC**

FOCUS
Means you concentrate better

SLEEP
Can improve sleep quality

CREATIVITY
Sparks ideas and new ways of thinking

Some people used to think that listening to classical music, especially Mozart, could make you smarter. Called **The Mozart Effect**, scientists discovered that people who listened to Mozart before taking an exam scored higher than those who didn't, although the effect only lasted for 15 minutes. Since then it's been shown that listening to music won't make you more clever, but it can have positive effects on your brain.

When The Mozart Effect was first talked about, people started playing children more Mozart. In the US, the state of Georgia even asked for money to send every newborn baby a classical CD.

In 2007, an Austrian dairy farmer claimed that playing Mozart's work to his cows made them produce more milk. He said he played the music to them while they lined up for milking. This made them calmer and happier, which meant more milk.

Italian vineyard Carlo Cignozzi says Mozart's opera *The Magic Flute* helped its grapes to ripen faster, which made them more alcoholic. They named the wine "Flauto Magico."

> — 66 —
>
> Melody is the essence of music
>
> **MOZART**
>
> — 99 —

FLAUTO MAGICO

A sewage treatment center in Switzerland has even claimed that playing *The Magic Flute* to its microbes makes them eat sewage waste faster!

PORKIE PIES

Mozart loved his food, especially liver dumplings with sauerkraut. He was also known to enjoy his pork and a new theory speculates this may have been the death of him. No one knows what really killed him, but written evidence proves he ate pork chops a little while before his death and if they were undercooked they could have given him an infection called trichinosis.

FEVER

Mozart suffered severe sweats.

RED RASH AND ITCHY SKIN

HEADACHE

A terrible headache meant he had difficulty moving his head.

NAUSEA

Vomiting and diarrhea made him dehydrated.

SWELLING

It started in his hands and legs and by the 14th day had spread to his entire body!

SYMPTOMS OF TRICHINOSIS

LIVER DUMPLINGS *with* SAUERKRAUT

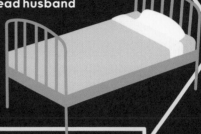

His wife Constanze was so distraught when he died, she climbed into bed with her dead husband so she could catch his illness and die too.

mozart *no pain, no gain*

After he died, thanks to all the mystery and murder rumors surrounding his death, Mozart's music became even more popular.

Experts have guessed at least

118 CAUSES OF DEATH

for Mozart, including
RHEUMATIC FEVER, FLU, TRICHINOSIS, MERCURY POISONING, AND KIDNEY FAILURE

DEAD END

On December 5, 15 days after the illness began, the world's greatest composer had a fit, fell into a coma and died.

† MOZART 12·5·91

> —66—
> I pay no attention whatever to anybody's praise or blame. I simply follow my own feelings
> **MOZART**
> —99—

SKULLDUGGERY!

At the time only the super rich were buried in graves of their own, so Mozart ended up in a community grave with no markings.

Every 10 years or so the bones of these multiple graves were cleared to make way for new bodies. A gravedigger who was supposedly a fan of Mozart's work made a note of where he was buried and, when the bones were cleared in 1801, he took Mozart's skull as a souvenir. It was passed down through his family who donated it to a museum in Salzburg in 1902.

GLOSSARY

AGE OF ENLIGHTENMENT
A special time in history when writers, musicians, and scientists came up with new ideas about politics, religion, and the way the world worked.

CLAVICHORD
A small keyboard instrument with a soft sound, perfect for use at home.

COMPOSER
Someone who makes up new pieces of music and writes them down.

CONCERTO
A piece of music written for a single instrument, accompanied by an orchestra.

HARPSICHORD
A keyboard instrument in which the strings are plucked, making a tinkling sound.

IMPROVISE
To make up music as you are playing, rather than reading it from a sheet of music.

MASS
A piece of music written to be sung by a choir.

MINUET
A piece of music written for a stately dance.

OPERA
A musical play in which all of the words are sung.

ORCHESTRA
A large group of musicians who usually play classical music together.

PERFECT PITCH
The ability to sing any note without being played one first as a starting point.

PIANOFORTE
An early version of today's piano, with fewer keys.

PRODIGY
A young person with exceptional talent or ability.

SMALLPOX
An infectious disease that gave you horrible blisters and killed thousands of people in the 18th century.

SONATA
A piece of music written for a single instrument, sometimes with a piano.

SYMPHONY
A longer piece of music written for an orchestra.

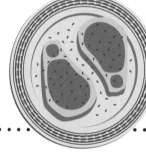

TRICHINOSIS
A disease caused by eating undercooked meat, especially pork.

Button Books

First published 2021 by Button Books, an imprint of Guild of Master Craftsman Publications Ltd, Castle Place, 166 High Street, Lewes, East Sussex, BN7 1XU, UK. Copyright in the Work © GMC Publications Ltd, 2020. ISBN 978 1 78708 060 7. Distributed by Publishers Group West in the United States. All rights reserved. No part of this publication may be reproduced, stored in a retrieval system, or transmitted in any form or by any means without the prior permission of the publisher and copyright owner. While every effort has been made to obtain permission from the copyright holders for all material used in this book, the publishers will be pleased to hear from anyone who has not been appropriately acknowledged and to make the correction in future reprints. The publishers and authors can accept no legal responsibility for any consequences arising from the application of information, advice, or instructions given in this publication. A catalogue record for this book is available from the British Library. Senior Project Editor: Susie Duff. Design: Tim Lambert, Jo Chapman. Illustrations: Alex Bailey, Matt Carr, Shutterstock. Color origination by GMC Reprographics. Printed and bound in China.